WHAT IT MEANS TO BE HUMAN

Youth Study Guide

Eileen
Campbell-
Reed

Produced in cooperation with
the Christian Education Ministry Group
of the Cooperative Baptist Fellowship.

ISBN 1-57312-089-8

What It Means to Be Human Youth Study Guide
Copyright © 1996
Smyth & Helwys Publishing, Inc.
6316 Peake Road, Macon, GA 32120-3960
1-800-747-3016

CONTENTS

INTRODUCTION

You hold in your hand a unique study guide. Usually a book study guide helps people learn about a book. This study guide, however, helps individuals integrate the ideas and concepts from the book into their everyday lives. The study guide is formed under four major headings—Guiding, Centering, Worshiping, and Responding. The Guiding portion of the book has three movements that provide the teacher with resources for group learning time. Each session includes activities that appeal to all types of learners. The Centering section offers the individual group member the opportunity to interact more personally and privately with the contents of the book. It engages the learner in reflection, providing opportunities for sharing with the larger group when appropriate. Worshiping is the section devoted to giving ideas and suggestions for corporate and/or individual worship opportunities. The final section, Responding, is designed to motivate the study group to action. It offers possibilities, based on what they have learned together, for putting feet to their thoughts.

Guiding

This part of the study guide invites the group to dialogue around five relevant issues or themes presented in the book *What It Means to Be Human*. The themes or issues are introduced in the form of a question. These questions are not necessarily related to specific chapters but are related to concepts woven throughout the book. This study guide is not intended to cover the book chapter by chapter. It assumes that participants have read the book in its entirety before beginning the study group.

Each session begins with an introductory page followed by three movements. The movements that shape each of the five sessions are:

SETTING THE STAGE
The purpose of this movement is both to introduce the question for the session and to help learners understand the relevance of the question to their lives and the world in which we live.

THE AUTHOR SAYS...
This movement is informed by the contents of the book and offers the learners an understanding of how the author answers the session question. It offers the learners the opportunity to struggle with the contents by looking together at several ways the book helps raise awareness around the question being discussed.

WE SAY...
This final movement invites the learners to respond to what they have read and learned. It provides group members the opportunity to consider how they respond to the session question. It is designed as an expressive movement, encouraging a response in some creative way.

Centering

These pages are for personal study, reflection, and discernment. They are reproducible for each member of the study group.

Worshiping

This section provides suggestions for use in worship that could be shared with the pastor and worship committee. Small group and individual worship possibilities are also provided.

Responding

This section promotes an active response. Possibilities for activities and projects for the group to participate in together are provided. Each suggestion supports the session themes in the Study Guide.

YOUTH LEARNING ABOUT
What It Means to Be Human

A major life task of an adolescent is to be a student and learn in school. Most of the learning in public (and private) education is expected to take place primarily through observing (seeing and hearing). This type of teaching is done with the methods of lecture, assigned reading, and repetition. Thus students hunger for learning in ways other than observing. They want to feel and do and even reflect at a deeper level.

One simple way to consider the ways youth learn is to think in four categories. Youth (and adults) learn by feeling, doing, observing (seeing and hearing), and reflecting. These four ways of learning are not independent of each other, but rather, they are like a cycle: learners must move through all four phases of the learning cycle in order to fully learn an idea or concept. However, it happens that learners tend to prefer entering the learning cycle at one of the four points.

As educators in the church, we must consider these dynamics, not only to overcome boredom and to offer more fun for youth in learning, but also for the sake of wholistic learning. By appealing to all the senses and to emotions, as well as to the mind, we will be teaching in ways that make a fuller impact on the lives of the youth we teach. This study is about the dignity, equality, creativity, and hopefulness of humanity. How better to teach it than to treat your learners with the attitude that they are well on their way to becoming fully human, and that they have as much to offer as human beings as you, their leader, do?

Most questions in this study guide are open-ended. Answers are not given in most cases because they lie within the learners. In some cases, the music chosen for the "additional activities" is quite thought-provoking and possibly controversial. If you choose this route, listen to the music for yourself and then use it as you see fit. You might use it as youth are entering the learning setting or as a closing, as well as for a discussion-starter.

Two proven ways of learning something new are to try it and to teach it. Keep this idea in mind as you plan to teach this study. While it could be done by one adult leader, it might be more effective when led by a youth and adult teaching team. You can be certain that the youth who learn the most will be the ones who help do the teaching. It takes a little more work to plan the study with a group, but the outcomes are worth it.

The five sessions are designed to be sixty to ninety minutes long. They may be longer or shorter depending on the size of your group. In several instances, options are suggested for younger or older groups of youth. In this book, you will also find suggestions for the setting of the study (see the Responding section), for worship to go alongside or as a conclusion to the study (see the Worshiping section), and for some individual learning and reflection (see Worshiping and Centering sections). You may put these suggestions together in whatever ways fit your needs with your youth.

As you begin making your plans, you will want to be sure to read *What It Means to Be Human* for yourself. You will also want to survey this study guide for ideas on how to flesh out the concepts for your youth. Any study or worship you lead will be greatly enhanced if all participants have also read the book in its entirety before the study.

GUIDING

Youth are just becoming self-aware, especially in the way they relate themselves to others. They are aware of right and wrong, and they know that they are capable of both. They may not, however, understand the inconsistencies in their lives.

Youth need encouragement to express themselves creatively. They are surrounded by pressure to conform to the fads and trends of the culture. At the same time, they are given messages to be self-sufficient and individualistic. These two messages, taken together, often meet in the form of isolation and depression. Youth need to hear God's message that we are to be ourselves completely and creatively, and to be ourselves in the presence of others. Healthy community allows its members freedom of expression with accountability and mutual love.

It is likely that youth in your group are often exposed to theories about human origins in school. These theories are most likely scientific and cultural explanations, not religious or theological explanations. Teens may have a difficult time reconciling the "what" and the "how" of creation with the "why" and the "who" of creation.

In this session, youth can learn that we are like God in relationships, emotional capacity, spiritual nature, creativity, and in our calling to nurture.

WHAT DOES IT MEAN TO BE Created in the Image of God?

Materials and Preparations

> Review the first two chapters of *What It Means to Be Human*.

> Obtain enough modeling dough for each member of your study group to have a one- or two-inch ball of dough.

> Obtain an easy-to-understand translation of the Bible, scotch tape, construction paper, markers, crayons, tape, and scissors.

> Cut out two large identical paper dolls from construction paper.

> Make three posters on newsprint or poster paper (or write on a chalk or markerboard in your learning area). Write one phrase per poster (leave room for a list under the two focus words): Remember where we came from: dustiness or dignity? Remember how much we've got to do: dominion or destruction? Remember how much we need each other to do it: design or desecration? Tape the two paper dolls on this last sign.

> Look over the options for a final activity under "The Author Says..."

> If you choose to do the additional music activity, obtain a recording of the suggested song.

> If you choose the arts expression, be sure you contact a leader well in advance and gather the needed materials for the project.

The Stage Is Set

If youth in this study do not already know each other, direct them to the construction paper, markers, crayons, and scissors. Invite them to make a name tag that expresses their individuality. Make sure you have a name tag as well. Encourage creativity with the name tags. You might suggest that they make their name tag in the shape of an animal that they wish they could be for just one day; or they might make their name tag on an enlarged first letter of their name (James would write his name on a large "J"); or they might make a name tag that includes all the nicknames that their family and friends call them.

Once the youth arrive and complete a name tag, invite them to sit in a circle on the floor, and give each one a mound of modeling dough.[1]

Begin by introducing the question, "What does it mean to be created in the image of God?" Be prepared to read the creation account found in Genesis 2:4a–4:25, but before you begin reading, say in your own words, **While I read, let your fingers be creative with the modeling dough. Don't think too much about what you are creating, just let your fingers find their way.** Then read the story slowly and with feeling. Pause when appropriate, giving the listeners time to soak in the words.

When you finish the story, ask the following questions, and allow time for the youth to respond to each question before moving to another. Encourage them in whatever answers they offer.

[1] If the season, weather, and setting allow, this beginning activity will have added benefit if it can take place outdoors.

Why do you think God took that much care in creating human beings?

How are people alike or different from the rest of creation?

How are we like God, in God's image?

After a brief discussion, say, **One of the ways human beings are like God is in our ability to create. What did your hands create while we have listened to the creation story?** Encourage each person to show their creations and tell something about what they made.

Say, **If one of the ways we are like God is in our creativity, what are some other ways? I'm going to make some statements. You tell me if they are true or false.**

> We are like God because we share a physical likeness. (F).
>
> We are like God because we are able to relate to God and others.(T)
>
> We are like God because we walk upright.(F)
>
> We are like God because we can hear and speak—responding to the world and God. (T)
>
> We are like God because we have the capacity to reason and we are intelligent. (F)

Take time to answer questions for the youth and explain what they need to know. Do not be concerned if you have to tell them that you are unsure about something they ask. Assure them that together you will search for the answers they seek.

· · · · · · · · ·

Say to the group, **In her book, Molly Marshall tells about a man in her first church who often prayed, "God, help us remember where we came from. Help us remember how much we've got to do, and help us remember how much we need each other to do it."**

Remember where we came from: dustiness or dignity?

Ask a youth to read Genesis 2:7.

On the newsprint or chalkboard, invite youth to write words or draw pictures of what comes to mind when they think of the dustiness of humanity—the earthy, sinful, temporary, and imperfect side of humans. Then also ask them to write what comes to mind when they think of the dignity of persons. Dignity is more than what people look like or the words they say. Dignity is the part of people that is genuinely good, loving, and willing to give of oneself.

Remember how much we've got to do: dominion or destruction?

Ask a youth to read Genesis 1:26-28 and 2:18-19.

To help teenagers understand how connected all of creation is, play the game "Wonderful Web." Ask for a volunteer to begin the game. Give the volunteer the assignment of being a cloud. He or she should stand in the middle of the room and act like a cloud. Ask the next volunteer to connect to the cloud as the next part of the web. For example, she or he would be a raindrop, snowflake, hailstone, or some other form of precipitation. This person should act like whatever is chosen, while at the same time touching the first volunteer. A third volunteer should connect in a similar way—as a tree, mountain, or lake that the snowflake hit and so on until everyone in the room has become part of the "Wonderful Web." This is usually a very energizing game, and you may want to play it more than once. Begin the second game with a different part of creation: the sun, the ocean, a bolt of lightning are possibilities.

Ask, **Because this web of life is so delicate, do you think God intended for us to "have dominion" by overpowering the earth? Why or why not?**

Can you think of ways that human beings have crossed over from having dominion and into destruction? (If they need help, you might suggest problems such as pollution, war, or mining without replacing the vegetation.)

Remember how much we need one another to do it: design or desecrate?

Ask a youth to read Genesis 2:20-24.

Say, **We were created by a God who wants our friendship and companionship, and because we are in God's image, we need that from each other too. But far too often, we forget how much we need each other. Instead we tend to cut each other down and hurt each other with our words, dirty looks, and harsh judgments.**

Take down one of the paper dolls and say, **This is our friend, Penelope Paperdoll. But she's not really our friend, because when we see her coming we snicker and make fun of her. Behind her back we cut her down, and to her face we tease her. I'm going to pass her around the room. When she comes to you, cut**

The Author Says...

her down and tear off part of her body—like this—**Penelope you are so ugly!** (Tear off part of her hand and pass her on around the room.)[2]

When she gets back to you (there may only be a tiny piece left!) say something like, **If we think our words don't hurt people, we need to think again. We all know it's true, because we all have been hurt by others. We all have felt like this. If you cut someone down enough, this** (hold up what is left of Penelope) **is what they look and feel like.** While holding Penelope, point out the other paper doll still up on the wall. Say, **She's nothing like she used to be. But we also have been given the gift of forgiveness to share with each other. So I want everyone to apologize to Penelope. I'm going to pass her back around the room** (in reverse) **with some tape. Say something to apologize and be kind to her, and then tape her back together.**

This process will likely take longer, and Penelope will never look the same. When she gets back to you again, say, **It was so quick and easy to hurt Penelope and tear her apart, but it took longer to try and put her back together again. Maybe you know what it is like to need to be put back together. Next time you are finding it easy to cut someone down to their face or behind their back, remember this picture.** Put Penelope back on the board next to the whole paper doll.

Continue by saying, **We need each other too much to be tearing each other apart and leaving scars that won't heal. Let's help each other to bear the image of God as it was**

[2] Ask everyone to keep the part of Penelope they tear off.

intended: creatively, relationally. And let us not destroy each other or our world.

The following are three options for additional learning activities. Read them and decide which will suit the group's needs in terms of time, resources, and interest of the youth. Gather the appropriate materials in advance.

OPTIONAL ACTIVITY 1

What about the dinosaurs? Engage youth in a debate between "evolutionists" and "creationists." Divide them into two teams and assign a topic to each group. The "creationists" should debate that the world was created in 6 literal, 24-hour days by a supernatural being called God. The "evolutionists" should debate that the world came into existence over millions of years and that there is evidence to prove it. Both groups may use Marshall's book, the Bible, and any scientific knowledge they can muster to wage the debate.

As you debrief the debate, help youth see that these two perspectives on creation address the event from two entirely different perspectives. The scientific inquirers want to know the "what" and the "how" of the world's coming into existence. The religious inquirers want to know the "why" and the "who" of the world's coming into existence. It is possible to answer both concerns with integrity. Help them to articulate their thoughts and convictions on this subject. If anyone gets too rigorous, insist that they take the other side for a while. That is a great teaching tool: by taking a different perspective, sometimes something more is learned about one's own perspective.

OPTIONAL ACTIVITY 2

What about my creativity? Invite a craftsperson to lead youth in making some item requiring their creativity. In advance, determine what materials will be needed and how long the project might take. The level of artistic ability should be attainable by all of your youth. Some possibilities might include the T-shirt project outlined in the "Responding" section of this study guide, a mural of creation, friendship bracelets, or hat art.

. . . .

Tell the story of Ernest in Nathaniel Hawthorne's *The Great Stone Face*. (You can find a summary on pages 49-50 of *What It Means to Be Human*.)

Ask, **What spiritual truth do you see in this story?**

How could you apply it to your life?

Being in the image of God is something we are on a journey to, and obviously we have not yet arrived. What does this story tell us about how to get on the right path?

Ask someone to read aloud 2 Corinthians 3:18.

Distribute paper and pens. Invite youth to write prayers to God. Some of them may never have written a prayer before. Explain that just as God hears our prayers spoken aloud, God also hears the prayers of our heart and the prayers we write on paper. Invite them to pray for some-

OPTIONAL ACTIVITY 3

What about the limits I put on God? Obtain a recording of "Color Outside the Lines"[3] by Glad, and play it for the group. Guide a discussion by asking the following questions: **How do you see God's hand in your life? How might God still be at work creating in your life? What limits do you put on God concerning how your life might be changed? How can you give God the "canvas" that is your life?**

one who has been on their minds, and to pray for themselves.

As a closing activity, form a "Sensational Circle."[4] Ask youth to form a circle facing inward and to stand close enough to each other to put their arms around one another's waists. Explain that you will move with tiny baby steps around the circle first to the right and then to the left. Anyone may yell, "stop," at anytime. At that point, the group will stop, and the person who stopped them should then share something "sensational" about someone else in the group. The affirmations should be about the uniqueness of the individual (and not just about their looks or their clothes). As you carry through the activity, be aware of anyone who has not had something "sensational" said about them. Be prepared to stop the circle yourself and affirm that person.

[3] This song is on the album, *Color Outside the Lines*, Light Records, 1995.

We Say...

[4] This activity is adapted from "Wonderful Circle" in *The Second Cooperative Sports and Games Book*, ed. Terry Orlick (New York: Pantheon Books, 1982) 90.

For youth, the primary tasks of work in their lives are going to school and studying. Many youth also have jobs around their homes, and some older youth work for pay outside their homes. They are considering careers, professions, and colleges. The choices can be overwhelming. Some feel pressure to perform, while others do not feel even the motivation to pass.

Younger youth are less focused on what they "want to be when they grow up," while older youth are increasingly concerned about what they want to do as a profession, and they usually have several possibilities in mind. One task we have in educating youth about work is to help all of them understand that no matter what we do, we can do it all to please God, from the tiniest detail to the largest project. Another task we have is to help young people comprehend that we are creative like God our Creator. Creating is a part of being in the image of God. Thus when we can do our work creatively, we are doing what God intended. We can bring creativity even to the simplest tasks.

Some of the work God has for us is to take care of the earth—creative work indeed! This is a calling we share with all the human family. Sometimes youth are better at remembering and acting on this calling than adults. Encourage their activity and give them opportunities to organize their efforts of caring for the earth. It is, after all, the only place we have to live.

WHAT IS THE Meaning of Our Work?

Materials and Preparations

> Enlist a panel of adults to discuss their work. Find three to five adults who have earned the respect of the youth and see their work as God's calling.

> Gather the ingredients for homemade pizza, and secure a kitchen near the learning setting in which to cook the pizza, using help from all the youth.

> Secure a chalk or markerboard and chalk or markers. You will also need some soft drinks and one empty bottle that had contained clear soda. Fill the empty bottle with water—very near to the top—and replace the lid. Remember which bottle it is because you will use it later to give the learners a scare when you shake it and threaten to open it.

> Write on slips of paper the jobs needed to make a pizza (see below). Place the slips of paper in a bag or basket.

> If you choose to do the additional music activity, obtain a recording of the suggested song.

> Gather paper and pencils for the brainstorming activity. Try to find paper that has been used on one side (but not with sensitive information on it).

> Make one copy of the brainstorming assignments and cut them apart so there is one per group.

> Look at "We Say…" and decide what you would like to do for a closing mission project. Gather the appropriate supplies.

The Stage Is Set

Say in your words, **Today we are going to explore the meaning of work. To help us start thinking about the question, "What is the meaning of work?" we are going to do some work. I think it will be some work you like. We are going to make pizza.**

Pass the bag of job assignments around to youth. They can be any of the following: dough mixers, choppers, fryers (if you have any raw meat such as sausage), timers, clean-up crew, assembly line for putting the pizza together, etc.[1] Take youth to the area where you will be cooking.

Items you will need: pizza dough mix, water, oil, (any other ingredients called for on the pizza dough package), pans, pizza sauce, pepperoni, onions, peppers, mushrooms, olives, other fresh vegetables, sausage, cheese, bowls, cutting board, knives, forks, paper towels, plates, cups, napkins, soft drinks, pizza cutter, and other utensils.

If making pizza seems too complicated, or if you do not have the facilities to do it, use a recipe that does not require cooking or refrigeration. (For example, you could make peanut butter and jelly sandwiches or fruit salad.)

[1] Adjust the number of jobs you create and how many youth will do each job according to the size of your group. Make sure all jobs are covered! If you have a small group, everyone may help with everything. For a really large group, you may need to have two complete crews.

After your food preparation and clean up are complete, talk about the experience of working together. Guide the discussion with the following questions.

Who just wanted to get this over with so we could move on to something else? Why?

Who enjoyed the work in and of itself as we went along? Why or why not?

Why or for whom did you do this work?

Were you able to express yourself creatively as you did your assigned task? How?

Do you believe work is a curse or a calling?

Read or quote Colosians 3:17, "And whatever you do, in word or in deed, do everything in the name of the Lord Jesus" (NRSV).

Depending on what type of pizza (or other food) you prepared, it may be ready to be eaten by the time you finish debriefing the experience, or it may be ready later in the session.

The Author Says…

Ask youth, **What exactly is your work? Right now, most of you don't have paying jobs, so what would we consider your work?** Allow time for youth to answer. You may want to write their answers on a chalkboard or markerboard. Encourage youth that the work they do now in school, learning and preparing themselves for a lifetime of work, is very important.

When the time comes to eat your pizza or other snacks, pick up your soda bottle filled with water and say, **There are a lot of pressures associated with working: time constraints, expectations from the boss and from yourself, being able to pay the bills…** While you say this, begin to shake the soda bottle a lot and move toward the youth as if you are going to open it. Then stop and open it where it would only spew on you. (Make sure you have the right bottle when you do this! And don't shake it too long, or they will catch on.)

After everyone has breathed a sigh of relief, say, **Sometimes what we think is pressure is really just some soothing relief! We only discover this when we look closer. Today we are going to take a closer look at the meaning and purpose of work. Here to help us do that are several members of our church who find more in their work than just a paycheck.** Introduce each panelist and tell briefly what they do as a professional or volunteer.

In advance, give adult panel members a copy of the book *What It Means to Be Human*. Ask them to prepare a three-minute talk about how they are able to see God's calling to them fulfilled through their work (professional or volunteer). You may include a paid staff member of the church on the panel, but it would not be necessary to do so. Explain to each panelist that they will be part of a panel discussion. Therefore, they will need to keep to their time limit and be prepared to answer questions from the youth.

It is important to help youth understand that God has a vocational purpose for them that fits their gifts and talents. This does not necessarily mean they will be called to be professional ministers, but remind them that all Christians are ministers and have a high calling to fulfill. They also need to understand that vocation and calling are more than a specific job; they are the thing we must do, because we can do no other.

When all the panelists have made their presentations, ask youth what questions they have for them. The following are some possible questions.

Was there a time when you felt called to do the work you are doing now?

How did you hear God speaking to you?

How did you prepare for your profession?

How does God use you in your work now?

Be sure to thank panelists for taking part in today's learning session. Encourage them to stay for the rest of the learning time.

Clean-up time. When the meal and discussion are over and it is time to clean up, ask youth if they know where the garbage goes—beyond the trash can! They may know more about recycling and taking care of the planet than you do. Divide them into groups and give them the slips of paper you copied earlier with the following areas to brainstorm solutions for taking better care of the earth—starting with our little corner. The facts and statistics in the brainstorming assignments are taken from Robert Parham's book, *Loving Neighbors Across Time.*[2]

> WATER—Think of all the ways you and your family use water every day: to drink, to shower, to flush the toilet. There is a lot of clean water being wasted by going down the drain every day. Come up with at least five ways we can cut water use in our homes and here at our church.
>
> HEAT AND AIR—Think about the places in your homes where the cooled or heated air escapes your house. And think about at least five ways you and your family could help cut back energy consumption used on heating and air.
>
> LIGHTING—Think about all the lights you have on in your house at any given time. Lighting uses 20 percent of all the electricity nationwide. How can we cut back on this power guzzler? Write down at least five ways to cut back and cut out our light use.
>
> RECYCLING—Paper, plastic, and aluminum are things we know can be recycled. In some places we can even earn

[2] Robert Parham, *Loving Neighbors Across Time: A Christian Guide to Protecting the Earth* (Birmingham AL: New Hope, 1991) 87-90.

[3] This may be a time when you want youth to begin planning their own "Earth Day." See the suggestions in the "Responding" section of this study guide.

[4] This song is on the *House of Love album*, A&M Records, 1994.

money for recycling these products. But what are other ways we can recycle by reusing and reducing in our everyday lives? Write down at least five possibilities.

When small groups have had time to complete their assignments, call them back to the large group, and ask them to share their ideas. Give everyone a pencil and piece of paper. Point out that the paper has already been used on one side. Ask them to write down the ideas as they are shared with the

group, so that they may put them to work in their own homes.[3]

ADDITIONAL ACTIVITY:

Consider playing Amy Grant's recording of *Helping Hand*.[4] Ask the following questions: **According to the song, who needs help? How can we help others even if it is not in a job description? Whose calling is it to help others? What can we do today?**

- - - - - - - - - -

We Say...

[5] Be sure when you send anything to an institution of any type that youth use the church address as a return address.

[6] If time does not permit working on the project together, send supplies home with the youth to complete.

Ask older youth to think about what each person in your group should pursue as a career. Ask them to think about how each person's talents and gifts and personality could be combined to make them capable of some particular job. If your group size allows, have each person become the center of speculation for a few minutes. Every other member of the group should be invited to say what they think this person could do well when he or she grows up. You may want to select a certain chair and get youth to take turns sitting in it, or you may just work your way around a circle. This can be a very encouraging and affirming activity for youth.

Younger youth have a more difficult time thinking that far into the future. Some of them have ideas of what they would like to be, but they may have even more difficulty coming up with creative possibilities for each other. As an alternative, you may want to try passing out paper and pencils to each youth. Ask them to write down their names at the top of the page. Then ask them to write three possible careers they like to think of doing when they grow up. When everyone has completed this part of the activity, ask them to pass the sheets

around the room. Each youth should read the others' papers and vote for the job they seem most likely to do. When the voting is finished, have them take turns telling the group the outcome of the voting.

As a closing activity, do a mission project that can be completed in a short time in the learning session setting and that provides an opportunity for the youth to be creative. The following are some possibilities: make tray favors for local hospital volunteers to place on meal trays, make and send cards to a nursing home or prison ministry, decorate place mats for a homeless shelter or feeding program.[5]

You and your youth will have your own good thoughts. Be prepared with some supplies and ideas, and let the youth decide how they want to carry out the project.[6] Set a date to deliver whatever you make.

Close with a prayer time. Invite youth to a period of silence. Ask them to listen for God's direction. Pray for each youth by name. It means so much for someone to pray for another aloud. Then invite youth to pray for each other and those to whom they will take their offerings of love and creativity.

- - - - - - - - - -

WHAT DOES IT MEAN TO BE Male and Female?

Youth are at a stage in life where they have become very aware of the different characteristics of males and females. They are also very aware of their attractions (and lack thereof) to each other. Their bodies are changing faster than they can comprehend, which creates insecurity in most. As adolescents begin to look less like children and more like adults, cultural expectations, as well as family expectations related to gender, become more obvious. Youth may find themselves complying with or struggling against these expectations, or they may be somewhere in between.

Youth have "win at all" cost so ingrained into their attitudes that breaking through to convince them that cooperation is better than competition will likely take more than this learning session. However, if you can help them enjoy and have fun at cooperative games, and point some of the ways in which fierce competition can be destructive to self-esteem, you will be on your way to helping change attitudes in your youth.

The games and activities are designed to accentuate the differences in males and females in the beginning of the learning session. You will probably not have to make much effort at escalating the competition, hostility, stereotyping, or double standards; the activities will do that on their own. Aim for a turning point at the time when youth study the biblical material. These activities may stir up some emotions that you will need to address later with individuals.

Materials and Preparations

> Obtain four poster boards, markers, Bibles, an apple, one chair, one hand-held mirror, a list of household chores (vacuum, dust, etc.).

> You will need two separate rooms or areas where two groups will not see and hear each other.

> Invite a man and a woman, each very secure in themselves and who treat the opposite gender with humility and respect and mutuality, to be facilitators for today's session. Tell them you will need them to observe how the boys and girls interact and then to share their observations with the group.

> Choose three different kinds of competition. Have the materials ready for the "Battle of the Sexes." Think of ways to play the games cooperatively so that you might offer the suggestions at the "cooperative" time.

> Make a large chart on poster board or newsprint, like the one in "The Author Says..." called "Ways of Relating."

> Make copies of the questions for the Bible stories for three groups.

> If you choose to do the additional music activity, obtain a recording of the suggested song (see below).

The Stage Is Set

To begin the session, say in your own words, **Today we are going to think about the questions, "What does it mean to be male and female?" and "How should we function as male and female?" To help us with this task, I have asked _____ and _____ to help us consider these questions. We will begin by dividing into two groups. You guessed it! Males and females.**

Explain that the two adults will be team captains and that you are going to have a "Battle of the Sexes." Introduce the three segments of the "battle." The following are some possibilities for competitions.[1]

TRADITIONAL SPORTS GAME: basketball, volleyball, softball, or soccer are good possibilities depending on the facilities you have available.

BOARD GAME: any game that involves competition and can be played in teams would be the most fitting for this phase of the battle.

BRAIN TEASERS OR MIND BENDERS: there are several of these types of games and books available in stores, or here are a couple of possibilities you may adapt:

• Numbers and letters in combination for common phrases or objects. You can make up many more on your own.

7 W of the W
(answer: Seven Wonders of the World)

8 S on a SS
(answer: Eight Sides on a Stop Sign)

18 H on a GC
(answer: 18 Holes on a Golf Course)

1001 AN
(answer: 1001 Arabian Nights)

12 I in a F
(answer: 12 Inches in a Foot)

• Bible trivia questions. You can make up more on your own.

What happened to Lot's wife?
(She looked back and turned to stone)

What did the spies look for at Rahab's house so as not to kill her family?
(A red cord hanging from her window)

What are the names of Noah's three sons?
(Shem, Ham, Japheth)

Jesus healed Bartimaeus of what?
(blindness)

Who were the two sisters that invited Jesus into their home?
(Mary and Martha)

What did Lydia make and sell for a living?
(purple cloth)

When carrying out the "battle," use timers, keep score, and put the pressure on to get the youth competing. Remind the adult facilitators to observe the behavior and speech of their groups. They may even want to write down their observations to share later.

With the group still divided into teams of boys and girls, give each team two sheets of newsprint or poster paper and markers. Instruct the teams to go to separate rooms with the adult leaders. The two adults should still be observing and taking note of the behavior and speech of the youth. Explain to the girls that they are to create a picture of the "ideal" male and a "typical" female. Explain to the guys that they are to create a picture of the "ideal" female and a "typical" male. Give the groups adequate time to complete each of their pictures, and then call them back together.

When they return to the large group, ask them to present their posters. Hopefully this will further illustrate the point of how our culture conditions us differently and expects different things of the two genders.

[1] If your group is large, you may only have time for one or two elements in order to make it through the other learning activities.

Introduce the "Ways of Relating" chart that you made in advance. Ask youth to set aside what they have experienced so far today, and promise that you will come back to discuss it further before the learning session is over. You may need to explain the meaning of some of these words, particularly for younger youth. You might even let them use a dictionary to look up the meanings of these words.

WAYS OF RELATING

competition vs. cooperation

hostility vs. respect

double standard vs. mutuality

stereotypes vs. equality

Then say, **We have gotten in touch with how males and females in our group can relate in ways that are competitive and even hostile, and we have seen how expectations can be stereotypical and full of unfair standards. Now let's see what God's intentions are and how some men and women in the Bible relate to each other. Don't worry; they don't always get it right either!**

Ask three youth to be readers. Ask one to read Genesis 1:26-31. Ask another to read Genesis 2:18-25.[2] Ask the third youth to read Galatians 3:27-28. After each reading, ask other youth to talk about the passage by comparing the "ways of relating" on the chart with what the scripture says. For instance, does the passage suggest we should work together as males and females—or be in competition with each other?

Divide the group into three smaller groups according to birthdays. Those born from January to April should be in a group; those born from May to August should be a group; and those born from September to December should be a group. If the groups are

terribly unbalanced, do some shifting, and if possible have males and females in each group. Distribute copies of the three case studies. Tell the youth they have ten minutes to read the story and discuss the questions.

SAMSON AND DELILAH

Read Judges 16:4-22

Discuss the following: To be people in love, these two sure didn't get along very well. Describe their relationship using the words on the "Ways of Relating" chart. How did Delilah show her hostility? Imagine how they would stereotype each other. (For example, Delilah might say that Samson is a "strong obnoxious type.") Would you say their relationship had a positive or negative outcome? Why or why not?

MARY AND JOSEPH

Read Matthew 1:18-25

Discuss the following: It was not socially acceptable to marry someone who was pregnant. In fact, Joseph could have had Mary stoned to death, according to the law. Yet he chose to listen to God and marry her. What do you think you would do if you were in his position? How do you think Mary felt about him? Using the words on the chart, talk about their relationship to each other.

PRISCILLA AND AQUILA

Read Acts 18:1-4, 18-19, 24-27;
Romans 16:3-5

Discuss the following: Priscilla and Aquila shared a unique relationship. It seems they worked together in their tent-making business, and there is also a possibility that she was from nobility (she was most always named first). Paul was a friend to them both. Considering the verses you read, how would you use the words on the "Ways of Relating" chart to describe their relationship? In what ways did they help Paul and Apollos? Could they be role models for how men and women get along? How?

The Author Says...

2 If youth in the group are very interested in drama, you may want to look at the suggestions in the "Responding Section" and get them started on some dramatic rendering of these passages.

Invite youth back to the large group. Let them report what they learned from the couples in the Bible. After the reports, say, **This is not just about how we get along in marriage relationships. This is also about how men and women work together, worship together, and treat each other in every setting of life.**

Ask for reports from the two adults who have been observing youth throughout the learning session. Ask them to recount what they saw from the youth by using the words on the "Ways of Relating" chart. Ask them to be specific with examples, and keep good humor about it. They can also speak from their experience about what works in relating to the opposite sex and what is not effective.

Ask for volunteers. You will need four sets of males and females.[3] Explain that they will need to use their most dramatic abilities.

IMPROV # 1
"One Guy, One Gal, One Apple":
Ask the pair to demonstrate hostility over the apple. There is only one, and they both want it. After a few moments stop the pair and tell them now to act with respect. Each of them still wants the apple badly, but now they should treat each other with respect as they discuss what they will do. Encourage them to find a creative solution.

IMPROV # 2
"One Woman, One Man, One Chair"
Ask the pair to imagine they are exhausted strangers because they have been waiting in an emergency room for hours and no seats have been available. Suddenly a chair becomes available. Role-play the situation using a double standard, as if only the other deserved to sit in the chair. After they have done this, ask them to act it out differently—this time with mutuality. Work to act with mutual concern for each other.

IMPROV # 3
One Groom, One Bride, One Mirror"
These two are newlyweds. They are staying in a cabin where there is only one tiny mirror in which to see to get ready (shave, make-up, etc.), and they have gotten up late. Ask them to act out the scene with competition as the defining characteristic. Then have them re-act it with cooperation as the driving force.

IMPROV # 4
"One Girl, One Boy, One Hour"
These two youngsters have been given a list of chores by their parents and must complete them in one hour or they don't get to go to the movie this afternoon. Play the first scene using stereotypes about who will do which chores (men's work, women's work, etc.). Play the second scene using equality about who does what—with the emphasis on getting the job done together and on time.

ADDITIONAL ACTIVITY

Obtain recordings of "Howard Grey," sung by David Burroughs,[4] and "Picture Perfect," sung by Michael W. Smith.[5] Play them for the youth and guide a discussion using the following questions.

How does the main character of each song see himself or herself?

How is your self-image as a male or a female influenced by the way others treat you?

What expectations do you think others have of you?

Have you ever treated anyone in a way that was hurtful just because he or she did not live up to your expectations?

What do you imagine this made them feel?

[3] If you have a small group, some individuals may need to do more than one improvisation.

[4] This song, written by Lee Domann, can be found on *Beyond Reason*, Colleen and David Burroughs, 1994. It may be ordered from Passport, Inc. (800) 769-0210.

[5] This song is on the album, *Change Your World*, Reunion Records, 1992.

• • • • • • • • • •

Now is the time to revisit the "Battle of the Sexes." Ask, **How could we play the same games as before but instead of promoting competition, and instead of using the same tired old stereotypes and double standards, promote mutuality, respect, cooperation, and equality?** Let youth think about how they could change the games they played earlier. Encourage them to use their imaginations. If they are having trouble thinking of ways to shift what they do, gradually add these suggestions to the brainstorming: change who is on what teams, play without teams, don't keep score, see if we can all get a collective high score, work together to get the answers, encourage everyone by cheering them on or patting them on the back, help each other to succeed, make our goal to have fun rather than to win at all cost, treat others as we would like to be treated while playing.

After they have come up with ideas for how to change the games you used earlier, reenact the games. They may even wish to rename the contest. Encourage everyone to have fun. When your time is up, call everyone to a circle. Debrief the experience by asking which way they enjoyed most: as a battle or in cooperative fun? Ask if anyone's view of how men and women should get along has been challenged or changed and if so, how.

Hold hands in a mutual way. If everyone will hold their hands out in front and turn their thumbs to the left, then take hold of hands next to them, then everyone will have one hand under and one hand over, which can be a symbol of equality and mutuality in your group. Invite youth to pray aloud for the person on their right and on their left as you pray around the circle. Close by thanking God for making human beings in such a wonderful way as to need each other.

We Say...

. . . .

Suffering and death are difficult subjects to face or try to understand. They are even more mysterious to teens who may not yet have had an up-close and personal experience with death. Youth are exposed to human suffering through the bombardment of the television and other mass media, yet they do not see or feel this suffering personally. However, you may want to pay attention to what tragedies are in the news in your local area at the time of this study. You may be able to personalize and humanize suffering with a real-life example by weaving it into the discussions when appropriate.

Most adolescents still believe they are invincible. They believe that bad things won't happen to them, and they rarely make an advance connection between actions and consequences. On the other hand, when trying to make sense of pain or tragedy, teens will also look for a direct cause and effect.

One of our tasks is to help youth understand that suffering can at times be the result of living in a world still under construction by God and not yet complete. At other times suffering can be the consequence of our human failures, and still other times it can be a combination of factors and thus beyond our complete comprehension. Youth need to know that even though God does not send suffering to human beings to punish them, it is okay to question God about the suffering they see or experience. They also need the assurance that God will not leave them during times of pain or suffering, but is present and ready to bear the pain with them.

Another task is to help youth face the reality of their own limitations including the fact that they will not live forever. The culture we live in does so much to help them deny their own limitations and death. Understanding how to live with awareness of death does not need to be a morbid reality, but rather it can help all human beings to live life more fully and more sensitively if they recognize the nature of human life.

HOW DO WE MAKE SENSE OF Human Suffering?

Materials and Preparations

> Obtain a marker or chalkboard or several sheets of newsprint, markers, glue, construction paper, a blindfold, and old magazines that may be cut.

> Make a "Feelings Poster": Using common emotions, draw simple faces that express the feelings. You may want to start with a "happy face" and make variations from there. Include at least the following feelings: happy, sad, afraid, joyful, ashamed, angry, depressed, confused, embarrassed, relieved, hurt, and shock. Display the poster in the room. When youth are having difficulty expressing feelings during a session, refer to the poster and ask if there is any emotion there that expresses the feeling about which they are trying to speak.

> Make cards for "Good News! Bad News!" (see below) by writing the situations on three-by-five cards. Tape them under the chairs in the room you will use for the study.

> Every participant will need a Bible and a pen or pencil.

> If you plan to have a guest share with the group, invite him or her well in advance (see "Setting the Stage").

> If you choose to do the additional music activity, obtain a recording of the suggested song (see below).

• • • • • • • • • •

The Stage Is Set

To introduce the question, "How do we make sense of human suffering?" play the simulation game, "Good News! Bad News!" Tape the following scenarios under the chairs you will use during the study: your best friend just committed suicide; you just found out you (or girlfriend) are pregnant; your parents just bought you a new car; your mother just died of cancer; you finally got the job you really want; you just failed chemistry for the second time; you finally got a date with the person you've wanted to go out with for months; you just got caught with drugs in your locker; you were just elected class president; you were in a car accident and the doctor says your legs are permanently paralyzed; you were awarded a college scholarship; your father had a serious heart attack.

You may add other scenarios or duplicate these if you have more youth in your study group. When youth arrive, ask, **How do you make sense of human suffering?** Be sensitive to the fact that some of the young people may have actually suffered significant pain or loss and may be at various stages of dealing with the experience. Allow youth to offer some suggestions.

Then tell them that to explore the subject of suffering, you are going to play a game called "Good News! Bad News!" Explain that each person in the room is about to receive some news that they are to share with at least three others in the room. Ask them to try and imagine what being in that situation would really be like. Direct youth to find a card under their chair. Allow them five minutes or more (depending on the group size) to mingle and share their news.

Following the mingling time, invite youth to debrief the experience. They may need to use the "Feelings Poster" to identify feelings they had while they played. Use the following questions to debrief the activity.

What was your first thought when you got the news?

How did you feel telling others this news?

What questions did you ask (or want to ask) about your situation?

What do you think was the cause of your suffering or joy?

If you were really in this situation, how do you think it would affect your relationships with family? friends? God?

Who was helpful to you?

What, if anything, made the situation worse or better as you shared with each other?

Another option for introducing this subject is to invite someone you know, and preferably that the youth know, to share from personal experience what it is like to live in a condition of chronic pain, extraordinary suffering, or other tragedy. It will be most helpful to ask a mature Christian who has lived with this experience for some time. If the pain is too recent, the person may not yet be comfortable is sharing with the youth. The debriefing questions above would be helpful in beginning a discussion with such a person. Keep in mind, of course, that this person had an actual experience, not a simulation; thus, sensitivity with your questions is important.

• • • • • • • • • •

Say in your own words, **Today we are going to spend some time considering the question, "How do we make sense of human suffering?" This is not probably on your top ten list of things to have a discussion about, but death and suffering happen all around us—and to us eventually. Death and suffering are connected. In the garden, God told Adam and Eve that if they ate from the tree of knowledge of good and evil they "would surely die." As you know, they did not die immediately. But they did live in a way that death and suffering were hovering nearby all the time. We also live lives in which death and suffering are present, but we find a lot of ways to avoid it and avoid thinking about it.**

Invite youth to help you make a list, on newsprint or a chalkboard, of ways our culture tries to deny death and avoid suffering. Direct them to look through magazines you have provided for advertisements and articles that point to this phenomenon. You may simply make a list as they take turns calling out their findings, or you may have them tear out their findings and tape them to the newsprint to make a collage.

Say, **The Hebrews actually saw death as a natural outcome of life. They understood that there was "good death" that came at the end of a long, full and satisfying life.** Ask one youth to find and read Genesis 25:7-8. Ask another to read Job 5:26. **Not everyone died a "good death," however; some died a "bad death," which usually meant it was premature. Sometimes "bad death" was seen as a result of violence or foolish living. Or it could mean that one did not have time to reach all of one's earthly goals.** Ask another person to read Proverbs 1:19. **As time went by, more and more emphasis was placed on the personal relationship between the individual and God. So the question came up, "What happens to my**

The Author Says...

relationship with God at the time of death?" This question was not fully answered until Jesus came and lived among us and died and was resurrected. Ask a youth to look up John 3:16 and read it to group.

Ask the question, **If Jesus Christ came that we might have eternal life with God, why is there still suffering in the world? And why do we still have to die physically?** Allow youth time to consider and respond to these questions.

The following activity is designed to help youth understand the concept that suffering has two primary sources: First, we live in a world that is still being created and is not yet complete; a delicate web of life is easily bumped out of balance resulting in natural disasters, disease, death and suffering. Second, some suffering is the result of human choice and sin. Finally, some suffering is a combination of factors in which blame cannot be clearly or easily determined.

Ask youth to take out the scenarios from earlier. First, ask them to write down who or what caused their "good news" or "bad news." Next, ask them to write questions they would ask God about this event in their lives. When they have had a few minutes to complete their writing, place an empty chair at the front of the room. Invite youth to imagine that God is sitting in the chair and that they can ask anything they wish to ask. Suggest that they imagine what God's answer to the questions would be. When one young person takes a turn asking the questions they have written, call on a different youth to tell what they imagine God's answer would be to that question.

As this exercise unfolds, you as the leader may have to interpret some misinformation or myths about God's role in the suffering of the world. It will be most helpful to challenge the youth with more questions. For example, if a youth says, "God caused my father to have the heart attack." Ask, "Does this fit with the idea that God is all-loving? What other factors may have played a part in your father's heart attack?" Help youth to think through the possibilities and understand that in many cases we cannot fully explain why tragedies happen, but that this in itself is not a reason to assume that God sent it (as punishment or otherwise).

To wrap up this activity, say, **We don't just have to imagine that God is here in this room with us and listening to our questions about suffering and death. God is really here! And God will not leave you, no matter what you face in your own life. If you will just reach out and ask, God will be waiting there to listen and respond.**

To introduce the idea of intentionally choosing to suffer as a response to God's call, briefly tell the story of Dietrich Bonhoeffer, and follow it with the activity below. **There is another dimension to suffering that is difficult for most Americans of any age to understand. It is the suffering that is intentionally chosen. And yet Christ, who suffered that we might live eternally with God, beginning now, also calls us to discipleship that involves carrying our own cross. There was a man who chose to take his call from Christ to discipleship very seriously during the second world war. Dietrich Bonhoeffer was born in Germany in 1906. He was a pastor and theologian who, in 1933, found himself very opposed to Hitler who was fast rising to power. He spoke out about his convictions in a lecture over the radio. The program was cut** short, and Bonhoeffer decided it was time to leave the country. He accepted a call to be a pastor in England. He not only opposed Hitler, he also thought the German Christians were compromising their convictions by not opposing Hitler. About two years later, he was called back to Germany to take charge of a secret seminary. While he was there in that tiny underground community of Christians, he also became convinced that it was a part of his responsibility to oppose Hitler by joining the resistance. This group made an attempt to assassinate Hitler and overthrow his forces, but the attempt failed and Bonhoeffer was taken to a prison camp. He spent the last years of his life in several prison camps and eventually was killed for following his convictions. Both in the secret seminary and in prison, Dietrich Bonhoeffer continued to minister to others and follow his convictions, which were to be the disciple Christ called him to be.[1]

When you have told the story, ask, Is there any cause you know about for which you would willingly put yourself in a position to suffer...or even die?

It is difficult for us to count the cost for taking on such a cause, but it is something we must consider if we are to be faithful followers of Christ.

If time permits, ask youth to form small groups and decide on a cause (child abuse, AIDS, world hunger, etc.) for which they would be willing to sacrifice or willingly suffer. Give them construction paper, scissors, glue, and old magazines; and invite them to make a poster/collage showing their cause. Allow each group to share their cause with the larger group and tell why they chose that cause.

ADDITIONAL ACTIVITY

Consider playing Billy Joel's song "We Didn't Start the Fire"[2] Ask the following questions: What is the "fire" in the song? Why do we try to fight it? Why will it burn on and on? What does this song have to do with the human condition?

[1] The information for this brief retelling of Dietrich Bonhoeffer's story came from the introduction in *Life Together* by Dietrich Bonhoeffer, translated by John W. Doberstein (San Francisco: Harper & Row Publishers, 1954).

[2] This song is on the album, *Storm Front*, CBS records, 1989.

· · · · · · · · · ·

For a closing activity, ask, Can we ever be ready to suffer or die? or live with a tragedy in our lives? (Pause for responses.) It is difficult to ever be ready for it, but there are at least two things that we all need to get through it. Do you know what two things I am thinking of? (Allow time for their responses.) The first one is God, and we have already said that God will not leave us alone in times of suffering and death. The second is each other. This would be the means for God showing us the care and love we need to help see us through the difficulties. Finding a trusting community to see us through times of suffering is difficult, so let's practice upholding each other with this game. Sometimes suffering and death are experiences in our lives that feel like we are falling with no control and no way to stop. We can, however, help cushion the blow for each other.

Form a circle standing shoulder to shoulder. Everyone in the circle will need to listen carefully to directions and cooperate for this to work. One person should stand in the middle blindfolded with his or her hands crossed over the chest touching opposite shoulders. Everyone in the circle should put their arms out, bent gently

We Say...

at the elbow, with hands facing the middle of the circle.

When everyone is ready, the person in the middle should fall back slowly keeping his or her body muscles tight. When that side of the circle catches the "faller," they should gently push him or her back toward the middle. The next persons to "catch" the "faller" should gently push. The "faller" will roll gently around the circle until he or she is pushed back to standing position. You may want to give as many of the youth as possible a chance to be the "faller."

Debrief the experience by asking youth how it felt to be in the middle, how it felt to be in the circle, and how the game might be like "being there" for a friend who is facing a difficult time, a death, or a tragedy. If someone truly falls during the game, and the group does not catch and support them, talk about how it feels to be let down and how it feels to let others down. Ask how they can "be there" for each other in little things now and how that might matter when big things come along later.

Ask someone to read aloud 2 Corinthians 4:7-12. Finish your learning time with prayer. Invite the youth to pray for each other and anyone they know who is dealing with pain, tragedy, or death. Thank God for always being present with us and being willing to hear our questions and concerns, no matter how difficult they are.

● ● ● ● ● ● ● ● ●

HOW DO WE FIND Hope in Christ?

Developmentally, youth should be at a stage in their lives in which they are learning about their own identity and are full of hope as they make plans and dreams for tomorrow. Yet for many this does not seem to be the case. Violence and crime are committed by younger and younger teens and even children. The statistics on teen suicide have continued to climb, which indicates a growing despair and hopelessness in the lives of our children and youth. Thirteen youth commit suicide every day, and hundreds more make attempts on their lives.[1] Even if you think this is not a factor with the kids in your church or ministry, you probably need to think again. Your particular youth may be in supportive and nurturing homes, but some of their friends are at risk.

There are two immediately obvious barriers to youth experiencing life and facing the future in hopeful ways. The first is the culture's conditioning toward instant gratification. Youth are so accustomed to having everything they want in an instant that they do seem to need to focus on the future. They lack understanding of what it means to wait for something they need.

The second barrier is the desolate landscape to which youth are exposed every day through the mass media. There has always been suffering, death, and destruction in the world, but now they can see it live and hear about it 24 hours a day on television, radio, print, and electronic media. When one hears about wars, famine, bombings, crimes, abuses, joblessness, and destruction of the planet all in the first ten minutes of the evening news, it tends to put a damper on even the most optimistic person's outlook.

Fortunately, Christians have been called to put hope, not in things of this world, but in Jesus Christ. Christians have also been called to offer hope to the hopeless. Youth need to be equipped to put their hope in Christ by understanding what scripture says, how hope functions in their lives, and what the promise of eternal life means.

As youth talk about the future and consider how they will spend eternity, some questions will likely arise about their relationship with God through Jesus Christ. You will want to be prepared to respond to questions for the group, and you will also want to follow up with individual youth who have deeper concerns. If and when they open a door, don't be afraid to help them walk through it.

[1] "Suicide," by Michael Warden, *Real Life Bible Curriculum: Senior High* (Loveland CO: Group Publishing, 1995) 1.

Materials and Preparations

> Write quotes about hope (see "The Author Says"...) on colored construction paper and place them around the room before the session starts.

> Obtain enough servings of pretzels, crackers, or other dry-tasting snack for each participant, a large bottle of cold water, cups for each participant, several Bibles, chalk, markers, scissors, glue sticks, copies of old magazines that may be cut up (some news magazines as well as beauty and home life would be good choices), and some paper towels.

> Write the following words on a chalkboard or poster before the learning session: anxious, hopeful, despairing, expectant, doubtful, anticipation, fearful, accepting, cynical.

> On a poster or butcher paper, at least two-by-three feet, make a chart like the one pictured in "The Author Says"..., leaving spaces under each scripture reference to write in key words.

> Enlist two or more youth to read the prayer of St. Francis. Give them copies in advance. They may read in unison or in parts that they determine.

> If you choose to do the additional music activity, obtain a recording of the suggested song (see below).

. . . .

The Stage Is Set

To begin, say in your words, **Today we will be talking about hope and the future. One way we can know if a person is hopeful about the future is whether or not that person can laugh in the present. Doctors, researchers, and the Bible agree on this one aspect of hope. They all agree that both healthy and sick persons can benefit from having some humor in their lives. Healthy people who find ways to relieve stress, including a good laugh, can help reduce the likelihood of getting sick, which makes the future look much brighter. When a person is ill, she or he can help the recovery process by finding the humor in something and by sharing a laugh with someone.** Ask a youth to read Proverbs 15:13 aloud.

Continue by saying, **Molly Marshall says in her book What It Means to Be Human, "Nothing helps us feel more hopeful about the world, and even about ourselves, than a good 'belly laugh' " (p. 141). So as we work our way through this study today, periodically I am going to ring this bell (or make noise with whatever noisemaker you brought), and the first person to raise a hand may tell a funny story or joke. You may tell something funny that happened to you. And please try to tell jokes that are not degrading to others.**

Remember to use your noisemaker several times during the session. You may want to think of a funny story about yourself to tell the first time you use your noisemaker so as to set the tone for what others tell.

Pass around the pretzels, crackers, or other dry-tasting snack to youth. Invite them to help themselves. Keep the bottle of water and cups out of sight in the beginning. Ask the questions below and keep the discussion going for at least five to ten minutes. During this time, your hope is that youth will become very anxious about getting something to drink. After they have all had some of the snack, get the water bottle out without saying anything about it. Just let it sit there, but don't open it or pour any. Keep passing the snacks around.

Guide a discussion using the following statements and questions. Begin by drawing the youth's attention to the words you wrote on the board earlier. Ask them to define the words with relation to the future. (The words are attitudes and feelings toward the future). You may ask them to give an example of how each word relates to the future.

Ask, **What is the hardest thing you ever had to wait for?**

Which of these words would describe your attitude or feelings while you waited? (Allow several youth to respond to this question.)

Generally speaking, who or what do you put your hope in?

Toward the end of your discussion, pour some water (and even drink some). Your youth may ask you for some at this time. Before you give them some water, add the following words to the poster or chalkboard: *instant gratification*. Ask if anyone can describe what these words mean.

Pour water for everyone and distribute the cups. Then ask, **How was waiting for water after the snack dried out your mouth like waiting for the future?** After they have had time to respond, read Psalm 23, putting the emphasis on the future tense of the passage.

• • • • • • • • • •

Is there hope for the future?

Invite youth to imagine their personal future by taking part in the following guided imagery. Explain that this is a means of learning and being open to God's spirit. For the best experience, they will want to relax while at the same time staying alert. To do this they need to follow your instructions. Speak in a clear, calm voice. Say the following, pausing at each "/," and a little longer at the "//."

Sit in an upright but relaxed position, placing both feet on the floor / breath deeply / with each exhale, blow out all tension and anxiety in your body / become aware of your body, starting with your toes and working your way up until you are fully aware of your physical being / now imagine yourself walking down a road / this is the road to your future; notice your surroundings / you come to a barrier in the road / what is this barrier and how is it preventing you from getting to your future? // now you are finding a creative solution to get past this barrier // now that you are past the barrier, what do you see ahead of you? / what is your future like? / where are you and who is with you? // once you have finished imagining your future, become aware of your surroundings in this room and open your eyes.

Debrief the guided imagery either by having youth get into smaller groups to share what they saw. Or if your group is small, allow everyone who is comfortable to share what they saw, what the barriers were, and how they overcame them.

In what do we put our hope?

Say, **As we saw earlier, one thing that reduces our ability to be hopeful about the future is that we have come to expect all our needs to be satisfied immediately and see little need to "wait" for anything. Another barrier that can prevent us from looking to the future with hope is the condition of the world around us. We are not the first in history to look at the conditions around us and despair.**

The Author Says...

Distribute five Bibles to youth and ask them all to find the book of Hosea. Explain that Hosea was a prophet who was called to proclaim God's message to the people of Israel at a time when they had begun to put their hope in things other than God. Ask them to look up the verses in Hosea and find things in which Israel had put their hope. Then ask them to write these things on the chart in the spaces you left under the verse references.

WHERE DO WE PUT OUR HOPE?

Israel	Us	God
Hosea 7:8-9, 11		Psalm 33:20-22
Hosea 8:4		Psalm 71:5-6
Hosea 8:5		Jeremiah 29:11
Hosea 8:14		Hosea 14:8
Hosea 12:8		Isaiah 44:2-3

When you have filled in the chart under Israel, say, **Where do we put our hope and trust other than God?**

Invite youth to look through the magazines you have provided to find pictures and words that represent things in which people in our culture place their hope. Ask them to cut out what they find and use glue sticks to attach it to the poster under "Us."

After they have had time to fill in that column, ask, **Which of these things or people, in the long run, fulfilled the hope people put in them? For the Israelites? For us?** Allow youth time to discover that everything on the list will eventually let us down (even friends, parents, church, military, government, leaders). Ask, **So where should we put our hope?**

Ask youth to take the Bibles and look up the verses under "God" and see what the Bible says about God and hope for the future.

What are your thoughts about the future?

Point out the quotes about hope that you placed around the room. Ask, **Based on what we have read in scripture and what you envisioned of your own future, go now to the quote in the room that says the most to you about hope. Read all of them before you decide.** When youth have had time to find the quote they like, Ask them to discuss with others who chose the same quote why they picked that one and why it is meaningful to them. If you have a smaller group, have youth bring back the quote they liked and share with the others their reasons for choosing it.

If hope were totally extinguished and there remained only despair, it would be impossible to go on living.
(John Macquarrie)

Lord, we know what we are, but know not what we may be.
(William Shakespeare, Hamlet IV.)

Go confidently in the direction of your dreams! Live the life you've imagined.
(Henry David Thoreau)

Life can only be understood backwards; it has to be lived forwards.
(Søren Kierkegaard)

What lies behind us, and what lies before us are tiny matters, compared to what lies within us.
(Ralph Waldo Emerson)

We live on the brink of disaster because we do not know how to let life alone. We do not respect the living and fruitful contradictions and paradoxes of which true life is full.
(Thomas Merton)

You must do the thing you think you cannot do.
(Eleanor Roosevelt)

*The greatest human quest is to know
what one must do in order
to become a human being.*
(Immanuel Kant)

*You don't get to choose
how you're going to die.
Or when.
You can only decide
how you're going to live.
Now.*
(Joan Baez)

*God grant me the serenity
to accept the things I cannot change,
courage to change the things I can,
and wisdom to know the difference.*
(Reinhold Niebuhr)

*Authentic hope,
as many contemporary
psychologists believe,
does not exist in a vacuum,
but rather in shared experiences
with others.*
(Molly Marshall, p. 141)

What will our future be like after death?

Say, **In our last learning session we talked about suffering and death, and today we have talked about some the barriers to a hopeful future. These are part of the human condition on earth, but what will be our condition beyond earth and death?** Invite youth to describe what they think eternity will be like. Ask youth to look up and read Romans 6:4 and 8:22-25.

When you talk about resurrection, children and youth have their imaginations to depend on. You may also hear concerns about body-soul dualism, which is a common belief. It is difficult for any of us to understand what a "resurrected body" will be like. But you may assure youth that our "souls" will not leave our bodies. Our souls include our bodies because a soul is the total and complete person. Thus, we will not be bodiless "souls" floating around for eternity. This discussion may also prompt some youth to want to talk about their own personal choice about following Christ in believers baptism. Be sure to follow up with these young persons.

ADDITIONAL ACTIVITY

Consider playing Bobby McFerrin's song "The 23rd Psalm (Dedicated to My Mother)"[2] Ask the following questions, **How did this song make you feel? Do you think God cares for you in this way (why or why not?) If you knew for sure that God cared for you this much, would it make you more hopeful? Why or why not?**

[2] This song is on the album, *Medicine Music*, EMI-USA/Capitol Records, 1990.

• • • • • • • • • •

Say, **We began by saying that humor was a sign of hope. Another sign of hope and a necessary part of our lives is our community of faith. We need each other to keep looking to the future.**

To introduce the game of "Knots," say, **Often we must work together to untie the difficult situations that make us feel less than hopeful. Let's play a game to express how we need each other.** (If there are more than 15 in the group, divide them into two groups for this game.) Everyone will need to stand in a tight circle, reach across the circle, take one hand in each of their hands, and then without letting go of any hands "untangle the knot." If anyone lets go, you must start over. The end result will be a circle with everyone connected to each other. Occasionally, the outcome is two or more interlocking circles. The game requires cooperation and encouragement, two things we need

We Say...

from others in order to face our future. Help youth to see this truth when they have completed the game.

When youth have made it into a circle(s), close your learning time with a prayer of St. Francis. Ask the youth you enlisted in advance to share the prayer. Or invite the entire group to say the prayer together.

PRAYER OF ST. FRANCIS OF ASSISI

Lord, make me an instrument of thy peace.
Where there is hatred, let me sow love;
Where there is injury, pardon;
Where there is doubt, faith;
Where there is despair, hope;
Where there is darkness, light;
Where there is sadness, joy.

O Divine Master,
grant that I may not so much seek
To be consoled as to console
To be understood as to understand,
To be loved as to love;
For it is in giving that we receive;
It is in pardoning that we are pardoned;
It is in dying that we are born to eternal life.

. . . .

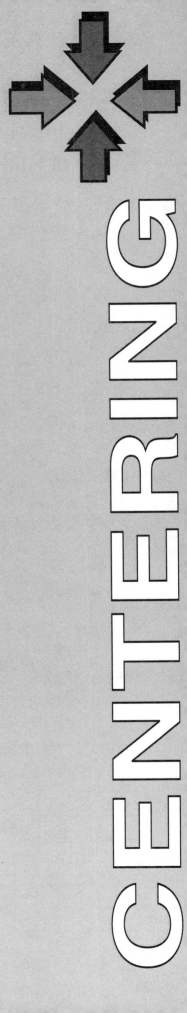

CENTERING

Centering on the Image of God

JOURNAL EXERCISE

One of the easiest ways to express yourself creatively is by writing down your thoughts, feelings, and experiences in a journal or diary. This practice has been used by writers, artists, and inventors for thousands of years. You will want a comfortable, quiet place to start. To begin, just write whatever comes to mind. Journals can be used to write music, poetry, dreams, plans, goals, prayers, ideas, stories, or just about the weather. It can be whatever you want it to be. A spiral notebook or book of blank pages may be used. Or you might prefer to write on loose-leaf paper and put it in a binder. You might include pictures that you draw or photograph. A journal can become a special way for you to express yourself. You can make all of it a prayer to God—because it is a part of you.

To help you get started on your first journal entry, the following are three possibilities:

Write about your surroundings. Describe everything you see, hear, and smell. Use descriptive words to tell about it. This is God's creation, so look carefully at all its wonder.

Write about yourself. What do you look like? How do you feel? What are your likes and dislikes? How are you like your family? How do you think you are different? What are your dreams for yourself?

Write about your day. What happened from the time you got up to the present moment? Who did you see and talk to? Where did you go? Did you learn anything? What was the highlight?

My Notes

_____

_____

_____

_____

_____

_____

_____

_____

_____

_____

_____

IN THE IMAGE OF WHO?

Find a mirror. Look at yourself. Answer the following questions:

Who in your family do you most resemble?

Who in your family do you most act like?

Who in your family do you most think like?

Could you say you are "in the image of" these family members? Why or why not?

You are also created in the image of God. In what ways do you reflect that image of God?

in relating to others?

with feelings?

with care of the earth?

DUSTING YOURSELF OFF

At times, most people tend to think too much or too little of themselves. Actually we are a strange mixture of dustiness and dignity.

In the space below, list ways you sometimes think too lowly of yourself.

Now list ways you sometimes think too highly of yourself.

Now read Romans 12:1-3.

What does this say to you?

Centering on the Meaning of Work

HEARING GOD'S CALL

Have you heard God's calling in your life? Everyone who has heard the call to follow Christ in baptism and then discipleship is also gifted by the Holy Spirit and called to act in the power of God's love in this world. Martin Luther said, "We serve God, we love God, we serve and love our neighbors in community, through vocation." We could rephrase the ending to say we love our neighbors by being together and doing our work.

As you try to hear what God is calling you to do, your vocation, there are so many things you can take into account. In the boxes below, write what you believe describes you in the areas listed. Then take the list to two or three other people you trust and ask them to add other things to the list—as they see you. This is part of serving "in community." It is not just that we give to others; it is that we receive from others and listen to their insights. Then we hear the voice of God more clearly.

Spiritual Gifts	Talents
Interests	Hopes & Dreams

. . . .

JOURNAL EXERCISE

Write a future story about yourself. Imagine that it is the year 2010. How old would you be? What would you be doing? What would a typical day be like? How is the world different than when you were growing up? What unusual event might take place in your life or career? How would you handle this strange turn of events?

. . . .

VALUING WORK

The following are some work-related values. Rate them with 1 being the most important and 10 being least important:

_____ dependability (be where you're supposed to be)

_____ punctuality (be on time)

_____ honesty (speak and act in truth)

_____ ingenuity (put your mind to a task)

_____ interest in others (act without selfishness)

_____ teachability (learn from others)

_____ followership (work well with others)

_____ creativity (figure out new and better ways to do a task)

_____ leadership (encourage and help others appropriately)

_____ initiative (act on own authority when necessary)

. . . .

My Notes

_____
_____
_____
_____
_____
_____
_____
_____
_____
_____
_____
_____

Centering on Male and Female

JOURNAL EXERCISE

For a journal entry, write what you like most about being the gender you are (male/female). Then write what you like least about it. What you would like to change about the expectations that the world has about your gender.

Write what you believe a perfect world would be like, if we were not plagued by the duality of humanity?

* * * * * * * * * *

DUALISMS OF ANOTHER KIND

We find many ways to separate ourselves in the human family: by the color of our skin, by our social or cultural roots, by the languages we speak, by gender (male and female), and by many other means. In what ways do you feel different or separated from others?

How do you intentionally separate yourself from others?

This week, how could you reconcile (bring together) yourself and some other person or group with whom you have been at odds? (Write a plan here.)

INTERVIEW A COUPLE IN YOUR CHURCH

Choose a couple whom you believe has a partnership marriage and interview them. You may want to use the questions below, and you may want to add questions of your own. Be sure to ask each spouse each question.

Names:

_____

How long have you been married?

How did you meet?
What was it like to date each other?

What three words would you use to describe your relationship?

How do you make decisions that affect you both?

How do you share jobs around the house?

How do you work out problems with each other?

How do you parent?

What do you do for fun?

What advice would you give to a person thinking of getting married?

My Notes

_____
_____
_____
_____
_____
_____
_____
_____
_____
_____
_____
_____

* * * * * * * * * *   * * * * * * * * * *

Centering on Human Suffering

PART OF A LONG LINE OF "LAMENTORS"

We are not the first people in history to suffer or to question God about our suffering. There is long tradition in the scriptures of offering complaints and questions to God about the human condition of suffering. A number of these "complaints" are written as poems called "laments." Many are found in the book of Psalms and in the book of Lamentations. Read Lamentations 3; then answer the following questions in the space below.

What feelings and emotions are found in this lament?

Which of these emotions have you experienced toward God? toward other people?

What were the events or circumstances that caused you to feel this way?

Notice how the lament writer goes back and forth between being angry at God and praising God. Describe a time when you were on an emotional roller coaster. What helped you to get on an even path again?

Read verses 19-27 again. Using these thoughts, write a prayer to God expressing your feelings—whatever they are right now—and remembering to thank God for being there for you no matter what your situation.

. . . .

JOURNAL EXERCISE

If you keep a journal (or if you don't, you may write on the back of this sheet), consider making the following entry: write your own obituary. Think about including information to answer the following questions. How old were you when you died? Did you suffer at the end of your life, or did it end suddenly? Who did you leave behind? Where did you live? What had you done with your life? What were your major accomplishments? What kind of a funeral service did you have?

. . . .

LOOK AROUND AND TAKE INVENTORY

Being honest about your own limitations is a difficult task when you are surrounded by media, and a culture, that values youthfulness and denies death and suffering. Yet we are also surrounded by death, tragedy, and suffering. Somehow we have learned to tune it out. Next time you watch television, make a list of the ways advertisements and programs deny the dustier side of life (for example: products that will help you look young, feel great, and attract the opposite sex).

. . . .

My Notes

_____

_____

_____

_____

_____

_____

_____

_____

_____

_____

_____

_____

Centering on Hope in Christ

HAVE A GOOD LAUGH

Molly Marshall says, "Humor, like grace, reminds us that we are imperfect persons to whom calamities and misadventures will inevitably occur. When we allow our laughter—especially our ability to laugh at ourselves—to accompany our bumbling incidents, it can be a healing balm for our need to be in control of all circumstances."

What was your most embarrassing moment?

Were you able to laugh about it?
Why or why not?

This week set a goal for yourself. Share some humor with others. Maybe you can tell a joke, a funny story, or just smile more than usual. Maybe you can see how many people you can get to smile in an hour, or a whole day.

My humorous goal for the week is:

My Notes

_____
_____
_____
_____
_____
_____
_____
_____
_____
_____
_____
_____

HAVE A GOOD LIFE

Now that you have come to the end of this study journey, maybe you will consider continuing to reflect on life in a journal. The exercises for this study have shown you a variety of ways to make entries in a journal. The possibilities are endless. You can write about the weather, your pets, your family, your feelings, a friendship, a past memory, a future hope, a dream you had last night, a plan you have for next week. You can include pictures and drawings and other art in your journal. It can become whatever you make it. And everything in it can be addressed to God and become the prayer of your life.

If you plan to continue keeping a journal, here are a few other tips. It will be easier to write everyday if you set a consistent time and place. Date each entry. Include your honest feelings. Go back and read your entries every once in a while. You will probably discover you have grown!

• • • • • • • • •

HAVE A GOOD LIST

Make a list of people who help you to feel good about your future. Include people who give you encouragement, people who inspire you because they have overcome difficulties, and people you know who just seem to make the world a better place.

Say or write a prayer of thanks to God for these individuals.

Then say a word or write a note of thanks to each person who is on your list this week.

• • • • • • • • •

WORSHIPING

Worshiping

Introduction

Involving youth as worship leaders is one of the most significant ways to teach them about worship and its importance. Some youth may never have served as worship leaders. As you help them to prepare to lead, consider these suggestions:

> Enlist youth to lead each part of your worship time. If at all possible, let them plan (or at least adapt) the service of worship. They will have more ownership and vested interest if they have been part of the planning as well as the service itself.

> Help them know and understand what they will be saying or doing; familiarity helps confidence.

> Practice with each youth worship leader severaltimes in the setting where worship will take place. It will build their trust in you as well as their trust in themselves to carry out the task.

> Explain that worship is not a performance for people who are spectators, but rather it is a drama played out before God in which all worshipers are participants. Leaders play key roles in the drama and set the tone for worship.

> Encourage youth to stand tall and speak from low in their bodies (not just from their throats). This will help them look and feel more empowered when they lead.

> Remind them that God really is present in worship and they should speak as if they are addressing God personally.

> Offer lots of praise and encouragement to each youth as they rehearse and lead.

You may find the following suggestions for worship helpful depending upon the setting where you find yourself and your group of youth. For instance, if you have chosen a retreat setting for studying this book, you may want to consider using the individual and/or small group suggestions for a time of worship while on retreat. If you are nearing a time when you have "Youth Sunday" in your church, you might want to consider the outline for worship that contains themes from the study.

INDIVIDUAL WORSHIP

It seems unlikely that teenagers would take the initiative on their own to set off into the woods or any other natural setting to worship God. However, you might be surprised at their responsiveness to such an invitation once they hear some possibilities. If you choose to include this option for youth in your group, it might be a good idea to set aside the time for them to (1) gather so you can introduce the subject, (2) go in separate ways for a certain amount of time to worship, and (3) gather again to share with each other about the experience.

Say, **For centuries some Christians have found solitary worship and meditation beneficial. In the years soon after the church was formed, men and women thought they needed to totally escape this world because it was evil and retreat into a wilderness setting to worship and pray at all times. Others formed "religious orders," which were groups who came together to live, work, and worship in a monastery or abbey where they were in a community of followers of Christ but separated from the rest of the world.**

As Baptists, we are in a tradition that values communities of faith that have regular contact with the world and are not separated. So this concept of individual worship may be foreign to us. However, some of the finest prayers, insights, and visions were written by those who were seeking God in solitude. There are some things we can learn from this tradition.**

Ask youth the following questions. **If you were to have a time of worship all alone, how would you spend your time? Where would you go? What would you take? Would you speak out loud?** Give each youth a sheet of paper and invite them to write down how they would worship alone.

Suggest the following items for youth to take to their time of individual worship: Bible, journal, pen, and possibly some appropriate music. They will need to find a quiet place to be alone. If weather and your setting allow, an outdoor environment would be ideal. Set a specific time for them to return to the group. Between 15 and 30 minutes would be appropriate depending on the maturity of the youth in your group. When they return, ask,

What was meaningful about your time alone with God?

How difficult was it to stay focused?

What was the hardest part?

Would you do it again? Why or why not?

SMALL GROUP WORSHIP

If you have a small group for whom you want to plan worship, you may want to consider adapting the ideas in "individual worship" or in the "worship outline." Small group worship can be an intimate experience. The greatest challenge with youth who are familiar and comfortable with each other is to make it meaningful. They may have trouble leading their peers in worship and be overcome with shyness or the giggles. Reverence and fun can go together—especially in a youth worship service.

Music will help greatly in setting the tone for a worship service. If you do not have a musician or instruments in your setting, consider using tapes or compact disks. There are some very fine recordings of contemporary Christian music available. Youth may be familiar with these recordings and be willing to share them with the group. And everyone has a voice and can make a joyful, if not perfect, noise in praise and worship of God.

If you are planning this service as part of a retreat or at the end of a study of *What It Means to Be Human*, your advance preparation can ensure that this will be a meaningful service, but be sure not to do all the planning alone. Involve the youth in planning. They will have some ideas about what they would like to do in a worship service.

Materials and Preparations

Items needed for worship:
> bread

> juice

> serving plate and cup

> basket

> pens

> an order of service for each participan, or at least the responsive readings printed on paper or written on an overhead projector.

Adapt this service to fit the particular needs of your group.

Call to Worship

LEADER: We remember where we have come from as we gather for worship.

PEOPLE: You made us, O God, from the dust of the earth, and placed us in a garden. You made us with your own hands and filled us with your very breath.

LEADER: We remember how much we've got to do as we pause for worship.

PEOPLE: You called us, O God, to care for your creation, to care for each other, to prepare the world for all those who will come after us.

LEADER: We remember how much we need each other as we draw together for worship.

PEOPLE: You created us, O God, to live in community, to celebrate each other, to work in partnership, and to uphold one another in all the seasons of our lives.

ALL: We make our remembrances an offering of praise as we worship you our Creator.

Invocation

O Lord our God,
      Creator, Redeemer, Sustainer of all life,
Open our eyes that we might see
      the everyday glory around us.
Open our ears
      that we might hear the sounds of creation's praise
As we worship,
      let us seek not to drown them out,
      but rather to sing in harmony with all that you have made.
May our worship and our lives
      join with creation's hymn of praise.[1]

[1] Peggy Haymes, *Be Thou Present: Prayers, Litanies, and Hymns for Christian Worship* (Macon GA: Smyth & Helwys Publishing, Inc., 1996) 26.

Hymn

Hymn "Come Our Sisters, Come Our Brothers"[2] (tune: Ode to Joy)

[2] Ibid., 91.

Prayer of Confession

God, you created us to be such a strange mixture of dustiness and dignity. We are reminded of our dustiness when we see those around us who are suffering and near to death. We are left without words when we see how lives can appear to be little more than dust in the wind—gone in an instant with no warning.

And yet we are equally amazed when we see the value of a beautiful life—full of dignity—a life like that of Mother Teresa or Dietrich Bonhoeffer . . . given so willingly for a higher calling. We human beings are such strange mixtures of dustiness and dignity.

Forgive us, O God, when we think we are all dust, unworthy and unholy, and swirling in the wind. And forgive us when we think we are too full of dignity, too powerful and too perfect, high on a pedestal. And forgive us when we are not able to love others in whatever condition they find themselves: full of suffering and near to death, or full of joy and high on life.

Help us to live in the tension between our dustiness and our dignity, aware of both, not overcome by either one. Help us to be present with others whatever their condition, with all humility and love. Amen.

Assurance of Forgiveness

Friends, believe the gospel! In Christ Jesus we are forgiven of our sins and cleansed of all wrongdoing! Your burdens have been lightened, so lift up your hearts to God!

Confessions of Faith

As a means of expressing your faith, you are invited to complete the faith statements.

* I believe in God . . .

* I believe in Christ . . .

* I believe in the Spirit . . .

[You may want to explain this way of confessing faith to worshipers in advance so they will be prepared to respond aloud at the appropriate time of the service.]

Hymn

Hymn "Let Us Break Bread Together" Let Us Break Bread

Communion

[For this time of communion, invite youth to circle the communion table or area. Offer simple words of instruction for the bread and the cup. Then explain to worshipers that you will pass the bread around the circle. Invite them to speak words of affirmation, blessing, or simple thanks to the person they are serving. Everyone should wait to eat the bread. When the bread has been passed all the way around, take the cup and pass it in the opposite direction inviting each worshiper to speak words of affirmation to the person being served. After each person has dipped the bread into the cup, she or he should go ahead and eat. Close the time with a prayer of thanksgiving. Explain that in the ancient tradition of the church, following the supper, believers would pass the peace of Christ. They may shake hands or hug one another.]

Offering of Selves

[Youth are not always in a position to give a lot of money to religious causes, but they are quite capable of giving of themselves in other ways. The "ushers" should first distribute paper and pens to everyone, and then a worship leader should invite worshipers to write down ways they can give of themselves to God. When they have had adequate time to do this, the basket can be passed to collect the "offerings." An alternative to this way of receiving the offering is possible if you have an altar area. Youth may be invited to take turns coming forward to write their "offerings" at the altar and place them in a basket there.]

Hymn

Hymn "The Servant Song" tune: Beach Spring

Benediction

LEADER: May you remember where you came from.

PEOPLE: We will remember.

LEADER: May you remember all that you've got to do.

PEOPLE: We will remember.

LEADER: May your remember that you need each other to do it.

ALL: The God of remembrance of hope will bind us together and go with us all the days of our lives.

. . . .

ADDITIONAL WORSHIP HELPS

Ideas...

BANNER

For the artistically gifted, creating a banner can be a wonderful expression of faith. It can also be an excellent visual reminder of your time studying *What It Means to Be Human*. If you choose to make a banner for worship, or for the youth area in your church, you may want to enlist the help of someone who has made a liturgical banner before. The possibilities are unlimited and thus can be overwhelming. You can do something as simple as giving each youth a variety of colored felt squares and some glue and asking them to create a picture of something they have learned during the study. Or you can become much more elaborate in designing and creating a worship banner that will last many years.

There are numerous books full of ideas for banners available at your local Christian bookstore. You need to determine a theme, and then work on a design. To make the design a reality, you will need to select appropriate fabric and trims. You will want someone who can help you craft the project in a durable and lasting way. Of course you will want to display the youth's creation in a place where it can be enjoyed by them and others.

DRAMA

In *What It Means to Be Human* , the story of creation is a focal point in nearly every chapter. If youth in your group are interested in drama, have them work on a dramatic presentation of the creation story. They may want to use music and dance to express the story, or they might write it into a reader's theater.

The drama could be done with one person alone, or a much larger group. If you have a large number of youth interested in this activity, divide them into two or more groups. Suggest that one group present the poem in Genesis 1:1–2:4a and the other group present the story in Genesis 2:4b-25. Yet another group could present the story of Adam and Eve's disobedience found in Genesis 3.

These dramas could be presented as a part of worship or as a culmination of the study itself. This is an excellent way for teens to express themselves creatively and to come to know the story more intimately.

SUGGESTIONS FOR
PROJECTS AND ACTIVITIES

The following are suggestions for taking the ideas and experiences from your study of *What It Means to Be Human* beyond the classroom.

Ministry Project

As youth discover more about what it means to be human, hopefully they may turn their concern beyond themselves to other human beings who are in need of God's love and concern. On the other hand, it may be that a ministry experience alongside this study in the classroom may be just the spark needed for true learning to take place. The idea of "service learning" is catching on in high schools and colleges across the country.

> Involve youth in each step of the process—from discovery of a need to evaluating the ministry experience. Their involvement in each step will help them to be invested in the project and find more meaning in it.

> Discover a need for ministry in your community. You won't have to look far. In fact, you will probably have to choose between several very needy situations. As you look, keep in mind the skills, gifts, and maturity of youth in your group. Be sure and ask youth what they are willing to do.

> Consider the following ideas[1] for a youth ministry project: take a party to an emergency children's shelter (often these children have never had a party thrown just for them); serve a meal to homeless persons through a local feeding program or homeless shelter; plug into an existing ministry in your area (for example, Salvation Army, Volunteers of America, and other community agencies often need volunteers for various projects).

> Determine how your group might meet the need. How many people will it take? What will they have to do? What special materials are needed?

> Set the time and place for youth to carry out the project.

> Prepare the youth by training them to do the needed ministry. Emphasize cooperation and teamwork as youth are training. Prepare them by asking them to pray in advance, as a group and on their own, for the situation and the people to whom they will be ministering.

> Talk with them about how a ministry project is different from any other community service they might do with the scouts or a class at school. Ask them how they can share the love of Christ with those to whom they minister.

> Carry out the project. Work alongside youth as you do the project, but also observe them as they do the work. Take note of who the leaders are, when someone goes beyond himself or herself to reach out to another person, and how the group grows in the process.

> Evaluate and debrief your experience. This step is critical to help youth make a connection between what they experienced in the project and their own life of faith. Ask them how they felt, what thoughts went through their minds, and how they changed as a result of the project.

[1] For other ideas about what types of ministry projects to do see, see Joy Bolton, *Ideas for Community Ministry*, (Birmingham AL: Woman's Missionary Union, 1993).

Get-to-Know-You Game

Play elbow tag. One person is "it" while all others in the game are standing in pairs with elbows locked. One other person (who does not have a partner) runs from "it." She or he hooks up with any pair before being tagged. Now there are three, so the person on the other end has to run from "it." If "it" tags the person being chased, she is no longer "it" and must then run and hook up with a pair. The person who got tagged is now "it." The twist: each pair standing together should try to learn as much about each other as possible while the game is going on. After some minutes of playing the game, have current pairs introduce each other to the group.

Have Your Own "Earth Day"

Part of bearing the image of God is responding to the call of God that we care for the earth. One practical hands-on way for teens to do this is to have an "earth day" in which they spend a day celebrating God's creation. Some of the activities you plan would depend on the season of the year. Any time of the year there are many places that just simply need to be cleaned up and tended to.

You might also consider starting a recycling project, planting flowers or trees, raking leaves, starting a compost, applying to your local community's government to be assigned an area of roadside that you would clean. For more ideas, see Robert Parham's book, *Loving Neighbors Across Time*.[2] As with other projects you start with youth, be sure they are in on the planning each step of the way. If they have ownership, they are more likely to follow through and find meaning in the experience.

[2] Robert Parham, *Loving Neighbors Across Time: A Christian Guide to Protecting the Earth*, (Birmingham AL: New Hope, 1991).

Youth Retreat or Lock-in

To retreat, or not to retreat? That is often a question asked by youth leaders and parents. A 1995 survey study revealed what impacts spiritual growth among youth.[3] The survey asked various questions about faith and spiritual growth to 1000 teens. In particular, responses to two questions offer some insight on whether or not to have a retreat. When youth were asked what was the most important factor in their deciding to become a Christian, their number-one answer was "a relationship with an adult Christian." When they were asked what one thing helped them to grow most as a Christian, their number-one answer was "participating in spiritual retreats."

Relationships crowded the tops of both lists, including relationships with parents and Christian peers, as well as Christian adults. Something special happens when a group gets

[3] Rick Lawrence, "What Really Impacts Kids' Spiritual Growth," *Group* 21, no.4 (February, 1995) 18-22.

away from the everyday humdrum of life and spends a couple of days focusing on their relationships with God. Some thing happens to the group who retreats together: they get to know each other better, and their relationships with each other grow. A better question might be, how can we not retreat?

The following is an outline for a youth retreat using this study guide. The first list is made up of things to consider while planning the retreat. A schedule is suggested below.

When planning a youth retreat:

> Determine dates, budget, and length for trip.

> Locate facility that fits the size of your group.

> Enlist adults to go with you; consider asking adults who could fill the roles suggested in the outline for the five learning sessions.

> Publicize the retreat and let participants know they will be expected to read What It Means to Be Human as their ticket to go (in addition to whatever cost you estimate).

> Plan your learning sessions well in advance, preferably with a team of leaders including some youth.

> Obtain all the needed supplies to lead the sessions and worship, as well as a few ideas for games.

> Duplicate "Centering" sheets for participants.

> Obtain a medical release form and parental permission slip from each participant under age 18.

> Have a great time—youl enjoy yourself most when you are well-prepared. Relax and enjoy the people sharing the retreat with you.

*Discussed fully elsewhere in this study guide

Possible Retreat Schedule:

FRIDAY EVENING
Get-to-Know-You Game*
Supper
Session 1: Image of God*
Break
Session 2: Meaning of Work*
Snack
Music and Fun
Lights Out

SATURDAY MORNING
Rise and Shine
Breakfast
Individual Worship*
Session 3: Male and Female*
Break
Begin T-shirts*
Lunch

SATURDAY AFTERNOON
Session 4: Human Suffering*
Continue T-shirts
Free time
Supper

SATURDAY EVENING
Plan worship for Sunday*
Music and Fun

SUNDAY MORNING
Rise and Shine
Breakfast
Session 5: Hope in Christ*
Break
Worship*
Lunch
Head home

Designing and Creating T-Shirts

As a closing activity or part of a retreat, guide youth to design and create T-shirts to help them remember the experience. Ask each youth to bring a plain white T-shirt to the appointed place and time. You should provide fabric paint, cardboard to insert in the shirts, and paper towels for clean up. If you use fabric paint, test out several kinds before you begin the project. Remember, the shirts will need to dry for at least 24 hours before being worn. Read the paint labels carefully. Invite the group to brainstorm ideas for the design of the shirt. (Here are some starters: "I'm only human!"; "Some of my favorite humans . . ."; "Being a human being is cool!" Your youth will be much more creative!)

You may go one of several routes with this idea. Every teen may design and create his or her own shirt—all of them would be unique. Or, the group might decide on one particular design and then work together to create the shirts. For example, they might form an assembly line in which Susie would write "human" in the same place on every shirt and Brad would draw a cross in the same place on every shirt, etc. Or, the group might decide on the same design and then all of them put it on their own shirts. Or, if you have a large group that is really into T-shirt designing, you could have the shirts professionally screen printed. Work with a specialist to get the design in a camera-ready form. Be sure you understand all the costs involved in having the shirts printed before you place the order. T-shirts make a nice reminder of a special event, and they give you a relational opportunity to bring up the event later and reinforce what was learned and experienced.

• • • • • • • • • •